The Palest Ink Is Stronger Than
the Strongest Memory

The Palest Ink Is Stronger Than the Strongest Memory

Trish Lenzi

ISBN-13: 9780692582671
ISBN-10: 0692582673

Introduction

My friend Dagmar and I went to her parents' home for a visit. Her mother is a sweetheart, but she suffers badly with Alzheimer's, needing to have someone with her around the clock. Her father is kind, but very depressed. He seldom speaks and basically lives in his armchair. I had brought *The Palest Ink*, a notebook with funny anecdotes I had recorded in a journal while our five children were growing up. I hoped reading these aloud might cheer Dagmar's parents up. I read a few pages, and they began to laugh. Suddenly, Dagmar's father popped out of his well-worn armchair and exclaimed, "Let's have an ice cream party!" Dagmar's jaw nearly dropped to the floor! So we had an ice cream party as I read the rest of the stories, and we all laughed.

The title of *The Palest Ink* comes from a Chinese proverb that says, "The palest ink is stronger than the strongest memory." So, having a lousy memory myself, I would immediately grab a pen and scribble in a journal anytime I wanted to remember something. All these anecdotes contain the actual words that our children said. Though I treasure looking through old photos, I find reading these stories even more interesting because they give a clearer "picture" of their growing personalities. We often read these on the kids' birthdays, on trips, or anytime we need a laugh.

So enjoy!

The second section of this book is a journal where you can record your own special memories. At the bottom of each page, you will find additional humorous one-liners from my children, just for fun.

Let's meet Joy ...

Like most first-borns, Joy got lots of loving attention. She started talking as soon as she was born and has never quit! No, but actually as a one-year-old, she would sing whole songs, word for word, as I changed her diaper. She was also very strong-willed and power-hungry, being totally fascinated with electric sockets. So we had our share of battles early on. But as Joy began to get older, she became quite a pleaser. For example, she would often slide a chair up to the sink and stand on it while she proudly washed the dishes. As the other kids came along, Joy became a second momma. She would play with the kids, read them stories with great expression, and even organize skits with make-shift costumes. Joy, with her bangs and straight, shoulder-length ash blonde hair, loved to dress up. But Joy would also correct her siblings, which they didn't appreciate, objecting "You're not my boss!" Joy was always a romantic. One morning in her kindergarten Sunday school class,

Joy got herself in trouble kissing the boy she was currently planning to marry, under a table!" Joy was a very cheerful child. One day my husband, Jonathan looked up the meaning of Joy's name in a name book. It accurately read, "Enchanted and enraptured with all of life." And I'll never forget my mom exclaiming, "How did you know to call her 'Joy'?!"

Joy's Memories

2 years old

One evening, Joy and her Daddy were taking a walk down the sidewalk in front of our third-floor apartment. Daddy pointed up and said, "Look, Joy. There's the moon!" They took a few more steps and the full moon was hidden by a nearby building. Once they passed the building, the moon reappeared.
With excitement, Joy pointed to the moon and exclaimed, "*Another* moon!"

❖ ❖ ❖

At a well-baby clinic appointment, a nurse was testing Joy's verbal skills. "Joy, see if you can fill in the missing words. 'The giraffe is tall, and the mouse is _____.'"
"Small," Joy immediately answered.
"Good, Joy, that's right," the nurse responded. "Let's try another one. 'The rock is hard, but the pillow is _____.'"
"Soft! I knew that one, too."
"Very good. See if you can figure out this one. 'Your mommy is a woman, and your daddy is a ____.'" Joy looked

at the nurse blankly, so the nurse rephrased the statement.

"'Your mommy is a girl, and your daddy is ____.'"

Suddenly, Joy confidently exclaimed, "*A boss!*"

❖ ❖ ❖

"What are you eating, Daddy?" Joy asked as she peered at his plate.

"Potatoes, carrots, and meat," he replied.

"That's not *meat*; that's *beef*," Joy corrected. "Can you say '*beef*,' Daddy?"

❖ ❖ ❖

While listening to the radio station, Joy always got very excited when she heard her name in a song. But this one morning, "A Mighty *Fortress* Is Our God" came on the radio, and Joy exclaimed, "Listen, they're singing *your name*, Mommy.

They're singing about *Trish*!"

❖ ❖ ❖

Driving past the toy factory where Joy's daddy used to work, I said, "Look, Joy, your daddy used to work here when you were just born."

Quite indignantly, Joy exclaimed, "You mean he wasn't with me?!"

"Oh, no, honey," I replied. "Of course he was with you when you were born."

"Oh, yes," said Joy, "I remember seeing him when I was in the manger."

3 years old

Preparing to leave our house, Joy explained to her younger sister,
"Christa, we're going to the bank to get a lollipop, but it will cost *a lot* of money!"

❖ ❖ ❖

On the way to bed one night, Joy shared, "Goodnight, Christa. I'll miss you while I'm sleeping, but I'll dream about you."

❖ ❖ ❖

One evening, our family was watching a televised basketball game together, and Joy fell asleep on the couch. "I'll carry her to bed," Daddy offered, as he gently scooped her up. After setting her onto her bed, he yawned, "Let's go to sleep, too."
"Sounds good to me."
But at 4:00 a.m., we were awakened by Joy, crying loudly. I jumped out of bed to check on her. "Joy, *what* is wrong?"

"You didn't read me a story!" she wailed. This same thing had happened one other night, and I knew there was no talking her out of it. So, I just grabbed the shortest storybook I could find and read it softly in the dim light, trying not to waken Christa as well. The minute I finished the story, Joy rolled over and fell right back to sleep. Traditions are everything!

❖　❖　❖

At breakfast, Daddy took a big bite of his jam-covered toast and commented,
"This raspberry jam really has a *distinct* flavor."
Joy disagreed indignantly, "This jam doesn't *stink*!"

❖　❖　❖

Beginning to notice some of the differences between the sexes, Joy informed us,
"Boys don't have boobies, they just have two pimples."

❖　❖　❖

After a rather long doctor's appointment, we came out to a hot parking lot. I opened the car door and a blast of hot air hit us. "Well, Joy, jump in."

But Joy had a better idea.

Totally serious, Joy proposed, "Let's get into another car that's not so hot."

❖ ❖ ❖

Our family walked into the gymnasium of a local junior college, looking forward to watching an interesting basketball game. "Kids, we'll sit here," Daddy informed them.

"Good. There's plenty of room in the bleachers for the girls to play," I observed.

Daddy lifted the girls over the second row where we sat down. A few minutes later, I glanced behind me, just in time to lean way over and restrain Joy's arm.

"I was just going to put this party hat on that lady," explained Joy, pointing to a well-dressed woman sitting to the right of us.

"Joy, that's not a *party hat*," I informed her, looking at the red and white striped cone she was holding. "That's a *dirty popcorn container*!"

"Do bugs have birthdays?" Joy wanted to know. "They probably do," I answered. "But I don't think they celebrate them."

Not satisfied with that explanation, she continued, "Maybe Daddy knows. I'll ask him when he gets back from work." Joy went outside. But I guess she couldn't wait to ask her Daddy because she hollered, "Jesus! Do bugs have birthdays?" Since no answer came down from heaven, I heard Joy conclude, "I guess He doesn't know either."

4 years old

We used to call Joy a little lawyer, because she would come up with an argument for all kinds of things. One afternoon she asked,
"Mommy, how soon can I start to wear mascara?"
"Probably when you're sixteen," I replied.
"Why not when I'm fourteen?" she argued.

❖   ❖   ❖

A friend of ours gave us some bookends of an old Jewish man reading the Torah. Joy took one look at the bookends and asked, "Are these *idols*?"

❖   ❖   ❖

Exhausted, I collapsed into an armchair, and Joy asked me, "Mommy, are you *exalted*?"

5 years old

"Thank you *so* much for writing down my story, Mom! And I *really* want to make up more stories," Joy shared as she climbed into bed.

"That would be great. But, for now, you'll have to be quiet so that you and Christa can get to sleep."

Lying on her back, looking up at me, Joy shared, "Thinking doesn't make any noise, does it? It just makes noise on my mind."

❖ ❖ ❖

"Look, bumper cars!" Joy exclaimed. "I want to go on them!"

"Oh, Joy, you're not tall enough yet," I informed her. "See that line above the painted clown?"

"Yeah," Joy replied.

"You have to be at least that tall to get on the cars."

Joy stood under the line asking, "Am I tall enough?"

"No, you need to grow about two more inches. Maybe you can get on them next year." When we got home, Joy, who hated naps,

made a very out-of-character suggestion,
"Why don't I take a nap? Sleep helps you grow, right?"
"Well…yes," I answered.
"If I take a nap, maybe I'll grow tall enough to go on the
bumper cars tonight."

6 years old

Daddy noticed that two-year-old Josiah suddenly appeared outside the girls' room. Then, their door quickly shut. Suspecting that Joy and Christa may be treating Josiah unkindly by excluding him, Daddy knocked on the girls' door. When Joy answered, he confronted her, "Did you push Josiah out of your room?"

"Oh, no," Joy replied. "I carried him out."

❖   ❖   ❖

Joy exclaimed, "Keith and I decided that once we get married, we're going to move to another country so we can become king and queen." (Joy didn't approve that the United States had no royalty.)

"So you and Keith talked about this?" I inquired.

"Not yet. I'll tell him about it the next time I see him."

❖   ❖   ❖

Joy had been asking me some of "the birds and the bees"-type questions. In response, I tried to explain, "Well, Joy, girls have eggs in them when they're born. But boys don't get sperm until they mature." That seemed to make sense to Joy.

Except, the next morning, I overheard Joy quizzing Christa, "Did you know that *mens* don't get sperm until they're *married?*"

Christa, with her never-wanting-to-be-outdone-by-older-sister syndrome, replied, "I know."

❖   ❖   ❖

As I walked into our kitchen, I was horrified to find Christa with her head tilted way back, trying to put a kitchen knife down her throat! "Christa! *What* are you *doing?*"

Removing the knife, Christa replied matter-of-factly, "I'm swallowing a sword."

"*You* know, Mom," Joy said. "We're acting out the scene from the Shirley Temple movie that we saw last week—the one where the man at the circus swallows the sword."

Oh, the effect of movies!

7 years old

As Joy was vacuuming the dining room, she noticed that her two-year-old sister Monica was afraid of the vacuum. In her typical, helpful, big-sister style, Joy assured her, "Oh, Monica, there's nothing to be afraid of. Watch this." Joy then lay down on the floor and let the vacuum suck up her long hair. Joy started yelling, and I came running and turned off the vacuum. It took forever to get her hair untangled from the roller. To top it off, we were in a hurry to go somewhere. And I'm afraid that Joy's trick didn't help allay Monica's fear of the vacuum at all!

8 years old

"When I grow up," Joy announced, "I'm gonna be a scientist and discover dinosaur bones and make a lot of money selling the bones!"

❖   ❖   ❖

Walking into the girls' bedroom, I found Christa lying flat on her back on the bed, with Joy bent over her, brushing her teeth. "Joy, what are you doing?"
"I'm the dentist!" exclaimed Joy with a big smile.
(And now she's a dental hygienist!)

14 years old

Frequently, our family would watch a movie together in the evening. But, oftentimes, Joy would fall asleep still sitting upright on the couch. When we would try to get her to go to bed, we also had to make sure that she took out her contacts. One night, while watching a movie, Joy fell asleep again. We told her that she needed to get up and take out her contacts. She just mumbled nonsense and resumed sleeping. Finally, Christa firmly commanded, "Joy, you have to get up and take out your contacts now!" Joy sat straight up, opened her eyes, and loudly announced, "I already put my tac nacks in my bibliography!" Then she leaned back on the couch and went right back to sleep.

Let's meet Christa ...

The night before Christa was born, my husband Jonathan and I still couldn't agree on a girl's name. We began reading Joy, 'The Very Hungry Caterpillar.' When we opened up the book to the dedication, it read, 'For my sister, Christa.' Both of us exclaimed simultaneously, "I like that name! If we have a girl, let's name her Christa!"

Christa was born at home with the assistance of an excellent midwife. While nursing Christa for the first time, seventeen-month-old Joy came in to meet her. Without a word, Joy climbed up on the bed, laid beside Christa and put her arm around her new baby sister. They've been close ever since, sharing a bedroom the whole time they lived at home. But at the same time, as Christa grew, she was very competitive with Joy.

Christa, with her straight, sandy- blonde hair and blue eyes, loved to be funny. One Christmas she dressed up like Santa, cotton-ball beard and all. She put antlers on our dog, Shadow, and on her little brother Aaron, and had him crawl on his knees. She had the other kids dress as elves. They paraded into our living room, where Christa, in her hilarious old-man-voice, handed out her presents.

Christa's Memories

1 year old

"Okay, Christa," I said as I lifted her out of the grocery cart. "You can get out for just a minute while I pay for our groceries."

"Your total is sixty-four dollars and thirty-five cents," the cashier informed me. As soon as I began to write the check, I heard Christa wailing loudly. I spun around in time to see an elderly woman pushing her grocery cart toward the exit, with Christa kicking and yelling on the bottom rack of this woman's cart! I ran over, stopped the lady's cart, and scooped up a very frightened Christa. "Christa, Christa, are you all right?" I asked as I hugged her tightly.

"Oh, my! I'm so, so sorry," the lady apologized. "I didn't even see her there." She fumbled through her purse for a scrap of paper and scribbled down her name and number. "Here, take my number. I'll pay for any injuries. Just call me."

"Thank you. But I think she's fine." Christa's wailing had subsided to quiet sniffling. I took the woman's number anyway and went back and paid for the groceries. Later, we all laughed.

What a way to steal a child!

2 years old

Christa knocked one of her little people toys over with another little person and then reprimanded, "Nanny! Don't knock Pappy down. That's not nice!"

"Hi, Keith," Christa said, as she gently patted her two-month-old cousin. "Oh, let me see him," Joy said, as she ran over and crowded Christa out. Shoving Joy out of her way, Christa asserted loudly, "Move over, Joy! *I* want to pet him."

❖ ❖ ❖

After bathing the kids, I decided to make some banana bread. Once I had the batter mixed, Christa noticed I was baking and climbed onto the chair beside me. She watched intently as I tipped the big metal bowl and poured the batter into a baking pan. Then Christa asked, "Can I have some?"
"Sure. Here's the spatula." Immediately, she got busy licking the batter out of the bowl with the spatula *and*

her little fingers. I popped the baking pan into the oven, but when I turned back around, there was Christa, grinning from ear-to-ear. "Christa Ann!" She had put the big metal bowl on her head like a hat. And, of course, she had slimed batter all through her just-washed hair!

❖ ❖ ❖

When we arrived at the grocery store, I lifted both Joy and Christa into the cart. I was feeling very organized because I had taken the time to rewrite my messy grocery list and had actually bothered to write the items in order of the grocery aisles! As I shopped, everything was going smoothly. "Well, we're almost done, girls, just two more aisles to go." I glanced in our cart. "Now, where did my list go?"

"Look, Mommy, Christa has your list!" Joy informed me. "Christa, Mommy needs her list," I explained as I gently pried it from her little fingers. "Oh, no!" I exclaimed. "Christa chewed off the bottom of the list!" And, of course, it was the only part I still needed.

❖ ❖ ❖

Christa came walking into the living room.
She was grinning from ear-to-ear 'wearing' one of our
little trashcans like a hat. Yuck! And what was even
worse is that she hadn't dumped the trash out before
she put it on. Double yuck!
Anything to be funny.

❖　❖　❖

While the girls were taking a bath together one evening,
I heard Christa say, "Joy, you're a good plugger."
"What does she mean by that, Joy?" I asked.
"Oh, she's afraid that the toys will go down the drain,"
Joy explained. "So she makes me sit on it."
"Why don't you just sit on the drain, Christa?"
I asked.
"Because it's not comfortable."

❖　❖　❖

Christa's routine for falling asleep was to hold my long hair with one hand and suck her thumb with the other. Several times one particular week, Christa had cried for me in the middle of the night because of bad dreams. By the third night, I finally asked, "Now, Christa, what *was* your bad dream?"

Christa sobbed, "I dreamed that I had nobody's hair to hold!"

3 years old

"Don't yell at me, Joy!" Christa hollered.
"I can yell at my own self!"

❖   ❖   ❖

"When God drops the snow down from heaven," Christa inquired. "Why can't we see His hands?"

❖   ❖   ❖

As I walked into the room where Christa was diligently drawing a picture for her grandpa, I asked, "How is your Father's Day picture coming?"
"Quiet, Mommy!" Christa commanded. "I'm writing a story." Looking over her shoulder, I saw that, above her drawing, she was writing all of the letters that she knew—about eighty *O*s, *I*s, and *T*s!

❖   ❖   ❖

It was Christa's fifth night away from her Daddy, because we were in eastern Pennsylvania visiting my side of the family, and he had to stay home and work.

"I miss Daddy. I want to see Daddy!" an overtired little Christa cried.

"I know you miss him, but you'll see him soon," I tried to console her. "Just lie down and rest. You've had a busy day swimming and visiting your cousins. Wasn't that fun?"

"Yes...but I miss Daddy," Christa fussed. "He needs to give me my goodnight kiss."

"We'll see Daddy tomorrow."

"But I need him *now*," sobbed Christa. "If only I could see just *one* of his eyes."

❖ ❖ ❖

At Christmas, we see relatives that we don't see the rest of the year. We were visiting at my in-laws' this one particular Christmas, when Jean, my brother-in-law's mother, scooped Christa up onto her lap. Christa turned her head toward me and questioned, "Mom, do I know this woman?"

"You met her here before," I assured her.

"Oh, yeah," three-year-old Christa said, turning toward Jean. "I met you when I was *little*, when I was *two*."

❖ ❖ ❖

"Mommy, look at the picture I drew!" Christa exclaimed. Pointing to the tallest person, Christa told me, "This is you." Pointing out the smallest, she said, "This is me." Lastly, she commented, "And that is Joy." Then, explaining the lack of the male members of our family in her picture, Christa continued, "Daddy and Josiah are still in your belly. They're still just eggs."

❖ ❖ ❖

Christa hated to take naps, especially since Joy had turned five and no longer needed to take them. One afternoon, when Christa was disgustedly getting ready for her nap, she surprised me with the comment, "I wish I were God."
Amused, I asked, "Why do you wish *that*?!"
"Well, because He never sleeps."

❖ ❖ ❖

"Hey, Christa," I said to her at bedtime. "This nightgown will fit you."

"I don't like it," Christa complained. "It looks like a dress, and you know I hate dresses. Do I *have* to wear it?"

"I'd like you to. It's cute," I encouraged. "Go ahead and put it on."

With a long face, Christa took the nightgown and trudged down the hallway to her bedroom. A couple of minutes later, she came skipping back exclaiming, "Now the nightgown doesn't look like a dress!" She had solved her problem by shoving the bottom of the nightgown into her undies!

❖ ❖ ❖

A few days after Joy had gotten sick to her stomach, Christa prayed this rather unusual prayer,
"Thank you, Lord, for Mommy not to frow up.
Thank you for Joy-dee not to frow up.
Thank you for Daddy not to frow up.
Thank you for the whole world not to frow up.
And thank you for God not to frow up.
Amen."

4 years old

"I like thunder," Christa shared. "Do you know why I like thunder? So I can practice not being scared of thunder."

❖ ❖ ❖

On our way home from church one Sunday, Christa informed me, "Mommy, when I have a baby I'm going to name it Mephibosheth." Poor baby!

❖ ❖ ❖

At 3:30 a.m., I was sitting on the living room sofa, nursing Monica. Christa came wandering out and shared, "I just had a scary dream."
"What did you dream?" I asked.
"I was having a birthday party, and Josiah opened one of my presents!"

❖ ❖ ❖

Due to morning sickness, I lost my breakfast one day.
Christa asked, "Are you sick, Mommy?"
"Not really, honey," I tried to explain. "It's just because of
the baby growing in my belly."
"Oh," Christa replied, "then it's just baby spit up"

❖   ❖   ❖

When she was little, Christa always hated to be outdone
by Joy. So, when Joy began reading and spelling, Christa
insisted on spelling as many words as she knew. It got a
bit ridiculous, though, one night as Christa was praying.
"Thank you, Lord, for M-O-M and D-A-D and J-O-Y
and J-O-S-I-A-H. Amen."

5 years old

Christa was zooming through her school books. (She had worked on them a bit the year before.) But she went ahead and finished her two kindergarten math books the second week of school. "Why are you in such a hurry, Christa?" I asked. "Are you trying to catch up to Joy?"

"No," Christa stated. "I'm trying to PASS her! Then I'm going to tell EVERYBODY!"

❖ ❖ ❖

After setting out the ingredients on our dining room table, I called, "Does anyone want to help me make an apple cake?"

"Yes!" the three older kids responded, as they ran into the room and jumped up onto the chairs beside me.

"Let's make the batter first, and then we'll cut up the apples."

"OK," they chorused.

"The recipe takes three eggs, so each of you can crack an egg into this bowl."

"Can I go first?" Christa asked excitedly, as she scooped up her egg. But she was so excited that she lost control of her egg, and it went flying over her shoulder and cracked all over the dining room floor!

❖   ❖   ❖

One afternoon, we stopped at the mall to pick up a few things. As we made our way through one department store, being very friendly like her daddy, Christa was cheerfully saying "Hi" to every person who walked past. Then we went past several mannequins, which Christa also said enthusiastic "Hellos" to. Then she turned to me and commented, "Boy, they have a lot of deaf and dumb people around here!"

❖   ❖   ❖

"Mom, it's so funny," Christa shared. "You're probably a hundred years older than me,
but I can whistle and you can't!"

❖   ❖   ❖

Not yet the geography whiz, Christa asked,
"What other countries are there besides Japan, West
Chester, Florida, and Hagerstown?"

❖　❖　❖

When I was pregnant with Aaron, Christa wanted to
know: "If the baby is surrounded with water, how can he
breathe?"
"Well, the baby has an umbilical cord attached where his
belly button will be. He gets oxygen from me through the
cord."
Then Christa asked, "If I attached a cord from my belly
button to yours, could I breathe through it?"

6 years old

While listening to a worship song, Christa picked up on the line, "His breath is in you." She questioned, "Is God's breath in us?"

"Yes," I replied, "It's in all of us who are Christians."

"And," Christa continued, "God's breath doesn't stink, does it?"

❖ ❖ ❖

"Mommy, I'm praying that you'll have another baby boy," Christa shared.

"Why do you want me to have another boy?" I asked curiously.

"So that Josiah can be rough on *him* instead of me!"

7 years old

Our family was at a baseball game when Christa walked
up and handed Josiah a small bag of potato chips, saying,
"Here's a treat for you."

Eagerly opening the bag, Josiah's face fell. He blurted out,
"This bag's *empty*! That was *really* mean, Christa."

"That *was* a mean trick, Christa," I corrected.
"Right now, I want you to go and buy him a bag of potato
chips."

"That's not fair!" Christa began crying. "That's *really*
not fair…Next thing you know, I'll have to buy Josiah a
house!"

Let's meet Josiah ...

As a toddler, Josiah was your typical rough and tumble boy. Training him to listen and to get along with his sisters took some work. To help motivate good behavior, I would give the kids a piece of candy if they hadn't gotten into trouble all day. One evening, Joy, Christa and Josiah were watching a video and I was just about to hand out the candy. Josiah was very excited that he was actually going to get a piece. But as I turned off the video, for just a moment, a boxing match flashed onto the TV screen. Totally unprovoked, Josiah turned around and punched Joy right in the eye! So much for the candy!

But Josiah, like his sisters, became kinder and more caring as he got a little older. He liked to be outside. Several times he found baby birds in distress and took care of them. Even when he was older and had started his own lawn care business, Josiah was kind to animals. One sunny day he was mowing a yard, but all these baby bunnies were getting in his way. He was afraid that he might run over them. So, looking for a solution, he found a concrete block, turned it on its side, caught all the baby rabbits and put them safely in the holes until he was done mowing.

Josiah, with his brown hair and blue eyes, was always tall for his age. He was extremely good at baseball and basketball and practiced those from a young age.

Josiah, as a young child was also my sweetheart. Our theme song was 'Once Upon a Dream' from Sleeping Beauty. I would turn it on and he would put his little feet on my big feet, and we would dance together!

Josiah's Memories

I year old

While Josiah was taking his first bath in the big bathtub, I noticed large bubbles coming out of Josiah's mouth. After careful inspection, I discovered he'd been chewing on the soap.
I confiscated the bar of soap and went back to bathing him, but he continued blowing big soap bubbles out of his mouth. I was baffled, until I noticed that he had a big chunk of soap stuck on his front tooth!

❖ ❖ ❖

I frequently caught Josiah on his tip toes grabbing things off the table. One evening, I went into another room before I finished clearing the dinner table, when I heard the telltale clunk of a glass. I went running into the dining room. There sat Josiah on the rug, holding a glass with a few sips of milk left in it, giving the cow and the donkey from our Christmas crèche a drink!

❖ ❖ ❖

"Watch out! There's a wasp!" I warned as I grabbed the fly swatter and began slapping at it and screaming.
I finally hit the wasp.
Then I scooped it up with a paper towel.
"Can we see it?" Joy and Christa asked.
"Sure," I replied. As I showed it to them, Josiah got up on his tiptoes, straining his neck, also trying to get a peek.
"I see? I see? I see?" he pleaded.
Lowering the wasp that was still twitching, I cautioned, "Be careful. It might still bite you." But Josiah must have misunderstood, because he immediately lunged at the wasp and tried to bite it!

❖ ❖ ❖

Like his daddy, Josiah loves to dip cookies in milk. But I found him coming up with some strange combinations. At a friend's house, I discovered him dipping his peanut butter sandwich in vegetable soup. And, to top that off, one day at his Pappy's house, I caught him dipping his cookie in his Pappy's glass of vodka!

2 years old

I was pleased that Josiah had gone straight to the bathroom after his nap. But, a while later, I couldn't find him in the house. So I looked outside and immediately spotted him. He was perched proudly up in a little tree, grinning at me. Only, he had forgotten to put his pants back on!

❖ ❖ ❖

Two of my older sisters, Evie and Sally, had to deliver their babies by C-section. Joy and Christa were aware of this and had asked if my baby would be pushed out or cut out. Josiah had overheard this, so several times he had come over and placed both his hands on my extremely large belly, pressed slightly, and commanded, "*Puush* the baby out!" One day, Josiah really surprised me by coming up and pretending to cut with his plastic scissors right by my big belly while saying, "*Cuttt* the baby out!"

❖ ❖ ❖

Monica was only six months old when Josiah begged,
"Mommy, please make *Monita* talk!"

Josiah had taken every single toy out of the toy box while
looking for his beloved gun holder. As soon as he found
it, he headed for the door.
"Wait a minute," I said. "You've got to put those toys back
in the toy box before you can go outside."
Josiah countered, "That's your job, Mom!"
Male chauvinism starts young!

❖ ❖ ❖

Josiah loved "shoot guns." He pretended all kinds of
things were his "shoot guns"—long blocks, rulers, sticks,
and especially my rolling pin. And, he was forever putting
his "shoot guns" in my pocket! (Did you ever try walking
around with a rolling pin in your pocket?!) Josiah usually
used his "shoot guns" to fight off pirates. One day, we
heard Josiah and Joy trying to play pretend together.
"*Lou* a pirate," Josiah asserted.
"Oh, no, I'm your wife," Joy disagreed.
"No, *Lou* a pirate!" Josiah insisted.

❖ ❖ ❖

I was working in the kitchen, when I heard Joy holler from the living room, "Mom, Josiah picked up Monica!" "Josi—," I started to yell, but then thought better of it, fearing that he might drop her. As I hurried into the living room, I found Josiah hugging his five-month-old baby sister, with his face just inches from hers. "Here you go," I said as I gently took Monica from Josiah and set her back into her infant seat. "Josiah, you're not big enough to pick up the baby yet. So if you ever pick Monica up again without Mommy or Daddy's help, I'm going to have to punish you. Now, Josiah," I quizzed, "what will happen if you ever pick Monica up again without permission?"

With a big grin, he replied, "You'll shoot me!"

3 years old

Josiah came leaping into the dining room, "Da-ta-da! Da-ta-da! Da-ta-da! I got dressed all by myself!" His pants were on backward, the telltale tag of his inside-out underwear was sticking out above them, and his shirt was on backward and inside-out. But he was so proud!

❖　❖　❖

Attempting to kill a fly, I joked, "Sit down, fly, so I can kill you."
Josiah corrected me, "Don't say that, Mom. Trick him. Tell him you *won't* kill him."

❖　❖　❖

"What's for dinner?" Josiah asked when we were visiting at my sister's country home.
"Fish sticks," I replied.
Extremely puzzled, Josiah said, "Fish sticks?" Then, it dawned on me that I had never served my kids

fish sticks. Josiah, still trying to figure it out, asked, "We're eating sticks full of little fish, like in the lake?!"

❖ ❖ ❖

"When I grow up, I'm going to marry you," Josiah announced to me.
"But how about Daddy?" I asked.
"I'm already married to him."
"That's OK. You can just have two Daddys."

❖ ❖ ❖

"Look, Mom," Josiah moaned, as he showed me his favorite racecar, broken into twelve pieces.
"Oh, my! What happened?" I asked.
"I couldn't get my car to work. So I threw it up high, so God could grab it and fix it! But it came right back down."

❖ ❖ ❖

Rocking in our rocking chair, I was watching Joy, Christa, and Josiah draw pictures on paper plates with magic markers. "The markers have smells!" Josiah exclaimed. He stuck his colorful paper plate right on my nose and asked, "Do you want to smell this?" (as if I had a choice!).

"Sure," I chuckled. "It smells great!"

Shoving his paper plate back onto my nose, Josiah repeated, "You wanna smell this again?" Much like his Daddy, who asks if you mind him doing something *as* he's doing it!

❖ ❖ ❖

"Mom! What are all these black specks in the ice cream?" Joy wanted to know.

"Oh, those are from the vanilla beans that they use to flavor the ice cream," I explained.

Christa walked into the room, picked up her bowl of ice cream, peered at it, and asked the same question. "What are these black specks in my ice cream?"

Josiah was ready with the explanation:

"Oh, those are the jelly beans."

❖ ❖ ❖

"Thank you, Lord, for this food," Daddy prayed at lunchtime. "And, Lord," he jokingly tacked on, "let Joy and Christa become as good as Josiah..." I peeked at Josiah to catch his reaction. Instead, I caught him taking a bite out of his sandwich while his hands were still folded in prayer! Mr. Angelic!

4 years old

While watching a Bible video in which a wingless angel
visits Peter in prison, Josiah commented,
"Angels don't have wings anymore. They used to, but
God pulled them off."

❖   ❖   ❖

Daddy had just put a flea collar on the stray cat that had
"adopted" our family. "I can't stand these flea bites on
my stomach," Josiah complained as he climbed into bed.
"They're so itchy.
I wish I had a flea collar like the cat!"

❖   ❖   ❖

For his fourth birthday, we gave Josiah a bow and arrow
set that he was very excited about. I carefully removed
all the staples from the folded target, trying not to make
the staple holes any bigger, and taped it to the refrigerator for him. Josiah studied the target carefully, and then,

noticing all the staple holes, exclaimed with disgust, "Somebody already shot this target with real arrows!"

❖ ❖ ❖

"Ew, look! A dead bird!" Daddy exclaimed, peering at the bird lying on its side in the grass.
"How do you know it's dead?" questioned Josiah, bending over to get a better look.
"Because it's cold and stiff," Daddy explained.
"When you die, will you get cold and stiff?"
"Yes," Daddy replied.
Placing his hand on Daddy's arm, Josiah said with concern, "Daddy, you feel pretty cold now."

7 years old

While watching the movie *Driving Miss Daisy*, Josiah, bewildered, asked, "How can Hoke (Morgan Freeman) be alive, when he died in the movie *Glory*?"

❖ ❖ ❖

"Her father *smacked* his lips after eating the birthday cake," Josiah read aloud from his phonics book.
Then he burst out laughing, exclaiming,
"Why is the father hitting his own lips?!"

❖ ❖ ❖

One evening, Josiah spent the night at his cousin Keith's house. They always had a lot of fun together. But, when they woke up, Keith's dad (Josiah's Uncle Frank) was parked in the house's only bathroom. So, the boys ran outside, jumped on their three-wheelers, sped down the hilly driveway, and raced into their grandparents' house to use their bathroom!

8 years old

Daddy came into Josiah and Aaron's room one night as
they were falling asleep. "Hey, Josiah…"
"Oh, Dad," Josiah muttered, half asleep,
"Don't talk. I only have a little time to sleep,
and I want to use it all up."

❖   ❖   ❖

Getting ready for his Little League game one afternoon,
Josiah asked,
"Can I have some money to take to the game, Mom?"
"What do you need money for?"
Josiah replied, "To use at the *confession* stand."

Let's meet Monica...

I was in the hospital for three days before Monica cooperated and decided to come out. A thumb-sucker from the start, Monica was actually born with a blister on her thumb from sucking it in the womb. Monica was a pleasant, happy child. She was petite and had very blonde hair. But if someone complimented her blonde hair, Monica would indignantly straighten them out, asserting, "It's not *blonde*, it's *white*!" Monica was a girlie girl, loving dresses and dollies.

Early on, my husband Jonathan and I began singing her a song from 'Fiddler on the Roof', but we inserted her name into it...

"Little bird, little Monica, you are such a sweet pretty little thing, everybody's fairy child. Gentle and kind and affectionate, what a sweet little bird you are, Monica, Monica, Monica." It's funny, but that song still describes her perfectly. Monica has always given everyone she knows a big hug whenever she runs into them. She's also quick to say, "I love you." As soon as she can, she'll go out of her way to help anyone who mentions a need. I would laugh at her because she's always had more 'best friends' than anyone that I have ever known. I never could convince her that a 'best friend' was only one person. Monica has always loved holidays. She loves to give cards and gifts, and, of course, she likes to get them too!

Monica's Memories

One year old

One evening, when Monica had just turned one years old, Daddy was watching her while Mommy was gone teaching piano. Monica was usually a pretty easygoing baby. But this particular evening Monica just kept fussing and fussing and fussing. In an attempt to cure her, Daddy stuck her in her crib and let her really holler. About ten minutes later, he let Monica out of her "jail" and set her back on the living room floor. Monica stormed over to the bookcase and angrily flung out every book she could reach! Revenge starts young!

❖ ❖ ❖

Monica liked to pull her Daddy toward her, using his ears as handles, in order to kiss him!

❖ ❖ ❖

One irritating habit of Monica's was that she constantly wanted to pull my eyelashes. While Christmas shopping, I spotted a baby doll with eyelashes and bought it. Monica opened her dolly Christmas morning and instantly fell in love with her, pulling at *her* eyelashes—so *I* got to keep mine!

❖ ❖ ❖

"Monica! Don't touch that!" her oldest sister, Joy, yelled. Monica hollered back, "Na, na, na, na, na!" Just like Christa and Josiah, who sometimes yell back at Joy, "You're not my boss!"

❖ ❖ ❖

Daddy had a way of making all kinds of little things fun. One way was he had this silly habit of renaming certain things. We used to buy these delicious little dinner rolls that he renamed "delectables." Our family was sitting at the dining room table, and Monica was in her highchair when she started fussing, "Bull, bull, bull, bull."

"What does she want?" I asked.

Christa figured it out. "She wants a *delectable*."

Two years old

Being a dog lover, Monica learned to say "Lassie" before she learned to say any of her brothers' or sisters' names!

❖ ❖ ❖

Daddy was being silly, acting like he was playing a violin. Monica asked, "Daddy, are you pretending to play the *vasoline?*"

❖ ❖ ❖

Walking into the living room, I found Monica sitting on her six-month-old brother's belly, rocking back and forth, singing,
"Rock-a-bye Aaron on the tree top…"

❖ ❖ ❖

Monica was our one child who would often rather play with her food than eat it. One evening, her daddy asked, "Monica, do you want some more hamburger?"

She enthusiastically exclaimed, "Oh, yes!"

"Will you eat it?" he asked.

"NO," she asserted!

Three years old

On our way to a doctor's appointment, Monica and I
walked onto an elevator, and Monica asked,
"Can I press the button, Mommy?"
"OK. Go ahead and push number three."
As we started going up, she got all excited.
"Oh, Mommy," Monica exclaimed. "I *really* like riding in
the *alligator*!"

❖   ❖   ❖

Watching a TV show one day, Monica saw people clang-
ing their champagne glasses together before they took
a sip out of them. "Mommy, what *are* they doing?" she
questioned.
"Oh, they're drinking a toast," I explained. But it wasn't
quite enough of an explanation.
Confused, Monica stated, "I don't see any toast!?"

❖   ❖   ❖

One evening as I walked down our hallway, I overheard Christa and Monica talking in the bathroom while Monica was taking a bath. Monica was asking her questions, and, to my surprise, I heard Christa explaining how babies come out! I stopped and stood by the bathroom door, curious to hear Monica's response. All Monica said was,

"That's tricky!"

Four years old

Making early plans for her future, Monica asked, "Mommy, when I get married, will you be my flower girl?"

Five years old

We rarely took our kids to restaurants, so I thought it would be a special treat to take Monica out to lunch for her fifth birthday. As we were enjoying our meals, five waitresses gathered around our table and began singing "Happy Birthday." Smiling widely, one waitress set a small cake in front of Monica with a single candle on it for her to blow out. When I glanced at Monica to see how she was enjoying all this, I was shocked to see that she was about to cry! She blew out the candle, and the waitresses went back to work. "Monica, *why* are you upset?" I asked, *totally* confused.

"Because…," Monica whimpered, "…they think I'm only *one* year old."

❖ ❖ ❖

Monica and her cousin Kathy, who was only nine months older than Monica, had been having a lot of fun playing together for hours. They had been using Buzzy, a toy that cuts shapes out of graham crackers. Then, they had decorated the shapes with colorful icing and sprinkles. After we left Kathy's house, Monica turned to me and asked, "Did you like playing with Kathy when you were little?" "Oh, Honey," I laughed, "Kathy wasn't born yet when I was little."
Confused, Monica continued to question, "But, Kathy's *older* than me?"

❖ ❖ ❖

"I just need one more nickel, and I'll have enough to buy a Creamsicle," Monica figured.
"Well, you can take a nickel out of our bank," I offered.
"Thanks." Monica opened the little door to our change bank and dug through the coins. Shutting the bank, she complained, "I couldn't find any put-together nickels, only pennies."

❖ ❖ ❖

Monica was in her room, trying on some of Joy and Christa's clothing that they had outgrown. After a while, she shuffled into our bedroom, wearing a pink flowered skirt, but gripping it tightly around her waist, she exclaimed, "Look, Mom, it fits me! But," as she let go of the waistband, "I'm too thin for it." And the skirt immediately dropped to the floor.

❖ ❖ ❖

"I need to stop in this store to pick up some wrapping paper," I told Monica as we walked through the crowded mall. So, we stepped into the discount store and wove our way around the tables, piled high with sale items. Monica grabbed something off one of the tables and exclaimed, "Look, Mommy!
Stick-on earrings! Can I get them?"
I turned around and took a good look at what she had in her hands. "Monica," I laughed, "those aren't stick-on earrings—they're *thumbtacks*!"

Seven years old

One morning Pappy called out, "Breakfast time! Come and get it." Everyone hurried to the table because they loved Pappy's cooking.

"Oh, yum!" Joy exclaimed. "Cheese omelets."

"And fried potatoes!" Christa added. "These look delicious."

"Everything looks great!" I exclaimed, as I buttered a piece of toast.

Monica sat down next to me and started eating. "Thank you, Pappy. This food is *so* good."

"You're welcome, Monica," Pappy replied. "I'm glad you're enjoying it."

But about halfway through eating her omelet, Monica turned to me and said apologetically, "Mommy, I just can't eat all of my *goblet*."

Eight years old

Monica was singing a song from *Fiddler on the Roof*, but she didn't quite get the words right, singing, "Who day and night must *strangle* for a living..."

❖ ❖ ❖

Monica and Aaron were eating raisins together,
and I overheard Monica say,
"We're having a raisin *party* so we can go *potty*!"

Twelve years old

"These birthday candles are cute!" Monica exclaimed, as she took a package of colorful candles off their hook and dropped them into our grocery cart.

"Yeah, they're nice," I commented. "Well, I think I have all the groceries I need. Do we need anything else for your thirteenth birthday party?"

"Oh, yes," Monica replied, pointing to the bags of confectioner's sugar. "We need a bag of *Confederate* sugar to make the icing."

Seventeen years old

Monica had saved up her money from waitressing to go with her Honor's English class to London and Paris. The first morning after arriving in London, their group was taking a bus tour through the city. Everyone was still rather groggy—groggy, that is, until Monica's announcement. Monica was studying the city out of her bus window and suddenly exclaimed, "Look, the signs are all in English!"

Everyone burst out laughing. "Duh, Monica, we're in England, and they speak English in England!"

Eighteen years old

Monica occasionally got teased for being an air-headed blonde because sometimes she gave evidence to support that! "Wow!" Monica exclaimed. "What a thunderstorm!" "Yea," I agreed. "Look at those branches swaying, and the lawn chairs blowing across the street!" There was an even louder crack of thunder than the last one that had made both of us jump. And, once again, the lights flickered out. "That's it," I decided. "I'm not taking chances. I'm going to disconnect the computer."

So I unplugged the computer and disconnected it from the telephone line. About twenty minutes later, the storm had subsided. "Hey, Monica, come on over and reconnect all the wires to the computer, so that you'll know how to do it if no one else is home."

"OK," Monica replied, as she crawled behind the computer desk. "What do I do first?"

"Well, first plug the power strip back in." She picked up the short, thick cord coming from the power strip. But, instead of plugging it into the electric socket on the wall, she plugged it back into itself!

Let's meet Aaron:

Aaron, who the doctor was concerned might come prematurely, ironically was born a whopping ten pounds. In his newborn photo his face was all squished up and he looked like a miniature boxer. Though he was the fifth child in our family, Aaron was not to be ignored. Frequently, as a young child, Aaron would grasp my chin and turn my face towards his, so I had to look right into his blue eyes and give him my full, undivided attention.

Aaron liked music and drama from a young age. One December day I had turned on a video of the Nutcracker Suite for him, then I left the room. A few minutes later, my husband and I walked into the living room to find Aaron squatting over his little white toy horse, swinging his plastic sword wildly, acting out the Nutcracker! I have taught private piano lessons for years at our house. Being a go-getter, by the time he was five, Aaron wanted me to start teaching him piano. Due to his young age, I was hesitant, but I reluctantly agreed to give it a try. It was definitely too frustrating for him, so I had him wait until he turned six. Then he took off, and in a few years passed the abilities of my older students. By the time he was in high school, he had become a better pianist than me!

Aaron, with his wide shoulders and muscular build, also enjoyed sports. Even as a little boy, he worked hard, especially on basketball. His daddy would help him, even having Aaron imagine certain scenarios as he practiced. One scenario they went over and over was, "Imagine it's the end of the game, your team is down by one and you're on the foul line. Make one for the tie. Make two for the win!" That exact situation presented itself when Aaron's high school team was competing in the semi-finals of the District 6 Championship. It was the end of the game and Aaron was on the foul line thinking, "Make one for the tie." He took his first shot. It went right in! "Make two for the win." Then he took his second shot. Swoosh. They won the game!!

Aaron's Memories

1 year old

After putting some groceries away in the refrigerator, I
turned around.
There stood Aaron on a chair at the table,
"helping Mommy with the groceries."
He was eating a raw egg, shell and all!

❖   ❖   ❖

Daddy was holding Aaron in church, when Aaron started
doing one of his favorite tricks, jamming his fingers and
thumb up his Daddy's nose!

2 years old

"Why are you two stabbing your Fig Newtons with pencils?" I asked.
"We're making Pop Tarts!" Monica and Aaron chorused, as they continued poking their cookies.

❖ ❖ ❖

I would give Aaron a gummy bear as his reward for using the potty.
One day, I gave him a choice, asking,
"What color gummy bear do you want?"
He cupped his hands together and replied, "A lot!"

❖ ❖ ❖

Our family was at a wedding reception, seated at a table with some other guests. I had Aaron seated safely right next me. I turned my back on him for a few minutes to talk to someone, when suddenly, everyone at our table started screaming. I whipped around, and there was Aaron, standing on his chair, holding a crumbled paper napkin over one of the decorative candles. Almost the entire napkin was on fire! I grabbed the flaming napkin, flung it on the floor, and, in my fancy dress and dress shoes, stamped all over it until all the flames were out!

Never a dull moment with a two-year-old!

3 years old

Our neighbor Dave noticed Aaron trying
to dribble a basketball on the road
and asked,
"So what are you doing, Aaron?"
He replied, "Oh, I'm *nibbling* the ball."

❖   ❖   ❖

Anytime we ran a bath, the water from our spigot
annoyingly drip, drip, dripped. Aaron was
taking a bath, and as the water incessantly dripped,
he exclaimed,
"Do you hear the music from the bathtub?!"

❖   ❖   ❖

I cut a peach in half for Aaron, and he exclaimed,
"Oh! It has *brains*!!"

❖   ❖   ❖

At eleven o'clock, Aaron climbed into bed and
announced, "I'm hungry!"
"Honey, it's way too late to eat now, but you can eat a big
breakfast."
"Now?" he asked.

❖   ❖   ❖

Aaron was unsuccessfully trying to get ketchup out of
an almost-empty plastic bottle but was only getting air.
Then he announced,
"Did you know that the ketchup bottle farts?"

❖   ❖   ❖

We were looking through packages of seeds at the grocery store. Aaron picked up a package of carrot seeds,
with a picture of a bunch of carrots on it, and said,
"Look! We can grow hot dogs!"

❖   ❖   ❖

One evening, Monica, Aaron, and I were lying in bed, taking turns making up stories. Monica went first, telling a cute story about a princess in a faraway castle. I went next, spinning an involved tale about a boy who kept telling lie, after lie, after lie.

"...Eventually, no one believed a word that boy said," I concluded. "Now it's your turn, Aaron."

Aaron immediately blurted out his story,

"A pig threw up!"

"Is that your *whole* story?" Monica challenged.

"Yes," Aaron replied. "A pig threw up!"

Monica and I shook our heads in disbelief, but then we burst out laughing.

4 years old

Aaron has always loved to correct and boss me around.
One day, when I happened to be squinting my eyes, he
commanded, "Mom, don't *squat* your eyes!"

❖ ❖ ❖

Aaron was helping me make applesauce, grinding the
cooked apples with our food mill.
He kept winding and winding and winding the handle
until he let go, complaining,
"Oh, my arm is getting dizzy."

❖ ❖ ❖

Monica and her friend Shawna were doing a puppet show
out on our deck. When Aaron came out, the puppet
show had already started. "Aaaah…" Aaron moaned with
disappointment,
"Did I miss some of the puppet show?"
"Yes," Monica and Shawna chorused.

"We're almost halfway through."

"Oh," Aaron pleaded, "would you *please rewind it* so I can see the beginning?"

5 years old

"The day before tomorrow Josiah got a lollipop from his bus driver," Aaron informed me.
"I wish I could go to school."

❖   ❖   ❖

We were watching the movie *Roots*, and the scene switched to an auctioneer rattling on and on.
Aaron observed, "They're fast-forwarding it!"

❖   ❖   ❖

Watching a jet with an impressive jet stream go by, Aaron exclaimed, "Wouldn't that be neat if they wrote my name in the sky?!"
"It sure would," I replied.
Aaron continued, "If they did, the sky would be mine!"

❖   ❖   ❖

I had made spaghetti with venison meatballs. As we began the meal, Aaron asked, "Is this a deer ball?"

"Yes, it is," I replied.

"Oh, good," he exclaimed,

"'cause that makes me jump higher!"

❖ ❖ ❖

I overheard the kids discussing some Bible stories.

"How about the story of Abraham?" Monica brought up.

"I think it's kind of sad," Aaron commented.

"What's so *sad* about the story of Abraham?"

Christa asked.

"Well," Aaron explained, "he got *shot* in the back of the head!"

I'm afraid Aaron got his biblical history mixed up with his American history!

6 years old

"Aaron, I think you're the sweetest six-year-old in the world," I complimented.
"And I think you're the nicest mom in the world," Aaron reciprocated.
"Thanks, honey! That's always nice to hear."
"You're sure nicer than Mrs. Shultz. She's so strict. She probably doesn't even let you pick your nose with a tissue!"

❖ ❖ ❖

Dad put flea powder on our new puppy Shadow, and Josiah began petting her. White flea powder was flying everywhere. Aaron came walking over confused, "*Why* is Shadow *smoking*?"

❖ ❖ ❖

"What is the 'First Lady'?" I asked Aaron during his oral history quiz. Aaron confidently answered, "The wife of the first president."

7 years old

Our family was at a track meet, waiting to watch Christa run. We were all sitting together, except for Aaron. After a while, Aaron came walking down the bleachers and sat down beside us. Joy asked, "So what have you been doing?"

"I was at the other end of the bleachers, watching them throw the biscuits."

"The *biscuits*?" We all roared with laughter!

"It's the *discus*!"

"Oh," Aaron said, embarrassed.

Then Christa, adding insult to injury, said, "Hey Aaron, did you hear that one of the competitors was disqualified because he took a *bite* out of his *biscuit*?!"

❖ ❖ ❖

One of my friends, Marie, came over for lunch one afternoon. "So what's your dog's name?" Marie asked Aaron.

"Shadow," he replied.

"Oh, that makes sense," Marie responded, "since she's totally black. And about how old is she?"

"Just one year old," said Aaron, "or seven years old in dog years."

"That's right," Marie replied.

"Wow!" Aaron exclaimed. "You'd be about *one thousand years old* in dog years!"

❖ ❖ ❖

Our family volunteered at a nursing home twice a month, reading current event articles, playing piano, and singing with the residents in their all-purpose room. Afterward, my kids and I would help them back to their own rooms, carefully maneuvering their wheelchairs down the long, cheerfully decorated hallways. One morning, after returning a resident to a room, I walked back into the large room.

There was my son Aaron with Grace, one of his most enthusiastic fans. They were laughing hilariously as he spun her in her wheelchair, around and around and around as fast as he could! Hoping and praying that no staff member was nearby, I raced over and stopped the spinning wheelchair. While Aaron and Grace laughed over who was the dizziest, I tried to explain to him that it wasn't a safe thing to do. "Aaron, Grace could fly out of her wheelchair and get hurt." His response? "But she *likes* it, Mom!"

❖ ❖ ❖

Aaron decided to make a Thanksgiving card, which he didn't want any help with, for his Uncle Al. He traced around his hand and made the drawing into a turkey. But on the inside, he had a little trouble with his spelling.

He wrote,

To: OWL

9 years old

During our history review, Josiah began reading the list of American presidents aloud, "George Washington…" Aaron blurted out, "Wasn't *Adams Apple*, George Washington's vice president?"

❖ ❖ ❖

Listening to a news report, we heard that John F. Kennedy, Jr. had died in an airplane crash over the ocean. Aaron asked, "Did they find his body?"
"No," I replied, "they just found some debris."
"Oh," Aaron questioned,
"was that the name of his wife? *Debris?*"

10 years old

During Aaron's first official basketball game, he took a shot and it went in. Then, he turned around and started running down the court, clapping for himself!

11 years old

Aaron was telling his dad about an interesting TV special
he had watched on the Olympic runner,
Jackie Joyner-Kersee.
Aaron mentioned several interesting facts about her.
Then he asked his dad, "Did you know that her parents
anteloped?"

15 years old

While Joy and her husband, Noel, were visiting, I was trying to get our rather noisy family to come to dinner. "Everybody up to the table," I announced, but no one paid any attention. So I made a megaphone with my hands and called a little louder,
"Everyone up to the table. Dinner's ready."
Aaron corrected me (one of his favorite things to do)
"Mom! Don't make a *xylophone* with your hands!"

Acknowledgments

I want to thank my family: Jonathan, Joy, Christa, Josiah, Monica, and Aaron; my friends Bill and Dagmar; and my sister Sally (our family's master storyteller!), who have always encouraged me with this project. Much appreciation goes to my mom, dad, and sisters Evie, Ruth, Sally, and Barb, who made my childhood so enjoyable. Special thanks to my mom, who created an atmosphere of family togetherness by making delicious dinners each evening, even served on a table complete with tablecloth, candles, and often flowers. We would talk, tell stories, and laugh.

I especially got assistance from my husband, Jonathan and my daughters, Christa and Monica, who helped edit *The Palest Ink*. Thanks also to Jonathan, Monica, Aaron and our friend, Dennis Angel for patiently helping me, despite my pitiful computer skills! I'm also grateful to my friend and former college roommate, Joy Thacker, for believing in me when I didn't believe in myself. I don't think I could have published *The Palest Ink* without her enthusiastic encouragement and writing advice.

Here's what our kids are doing currently:

Joy Elizabeth Handran, thirty-three years old, is a part-time dental hygienist and full-time mother of three: seven-year-old Elley, five-year-old Everett, and one-year-old Cameron. Her husband, Noel, is a fifth grade teacher and a super helpful husband and dad. Joy is an excellent home decorator. She is also very cheerful, generous, and goes out of her way to bless others.

Christa Ann Lenzi, thirty-one years old, is a clinical pharmacist in a hospital. She works in the intensive care unit and is a well-liked and respected aid to the surgeons and nurses there. She likes to work out. Being quite artistic, Christa has very creatively decorated her apartment. Christa is also very generous and outrageously funny!

Josiah James Lenzi, twenty-nine years old, is a finance manager at a large car dealership. He recently married Olivia Griffith, who is very friendly and cheerful. They planned a beautiful wedding. Then, on their honeymoon, they went to Jamaica and even got to swim with dolphins! Josiah is good at art and basketball. He is also kind, helpful, generous, and hard-working.

Monica Lynn Truitt, twenty-seven years old, is a guidance counselor. Monica is very kind, cheerful, and helpful. She still loves holidays and gives great cards and gifts. She's married to Josh, who is a talented chef and likes to cook at home! They have a little girl named Madilyn who just learned to walk. She loves to smile, laugh, and give open-mouth kisses!

Aaron Michael Lenzi, twenty-five years old, is extremely good at mathematics and is a mechanical engineer. Aaron is hard-working, caring, generous, and pleasant. He likes to play baseball, basketball, and volleyball. Aaron is also a very gifted artist, pianist, and singer. He's very friendly and likeable and is great with kids!

The Palest Ink
Journal

The perfect place to record your
own special memories!

Trish Lenzi

Introduction

Were you inspired by *The Palest Ink*? This journal is the perfect place to record your own funny or special memories! You could record humorous things your children or grandchildren have said or done, things which are so easily forgotten. My oldest daughter, Joy, works part-time, her husband, Noel, works full-time, and they have three young children. Even in their hectic lives, they have been able to continue this tradition of jotting down funny and special memories. They've come up with a habit of scribbling down the gist of a memory in shorthand on their calendar. Then, later, when they have more time, they write the anecdotes out more legibly into a journal. Maybe that method will work for you.

Another option would be to use this journal to write down pleasant memories from your own childhood and possibly your parents' or grandparents' past. It's a great way to pass along family stories! These memories are so much fun to read and reread or to share at family gatherings. Laughter creates a pleasant atmosphere and bonds people together.

So scribble away and enjoy!

*While feeling her elbow, Monica announced,
"I have an ankle on my arm!"*

_____
_____
_____
_____
_____
_____
_____
_____
_____
_____
_____
_____
_____
_____
_____
_____
_____
_____
_____
_____
_____

Aaron asked, "Mom, would you be a gentleman
and open the door for me?"

_____
_____
_____
_____
_____
_____
_____
_____
_____
_____
_____
_____
_____
_____
_____
_____
_____
_____
_____
_____

Clenching her fists playfully, Christa demanded,
"Whobody took my crayons?"

_"Mommy," Monica requested, "will you teach
me how to count my BACs?"_

Noticing a whole bunch of flies
sitting on home base, Aaron asked,
"Did you notice that flock of flies on home base?"

Joy picked up a sesame seed that had fallen off her cracker and questioned seriously,
"If I plant this seed, will it grow crackers?"

We found one-year-old Josiah, who loved to get a laugh, grinning from ear to ear, while brushing his toes with his toothbrush!

Aaron was looking at a digital clock that read 7:00 and informed us,
"It's seven hundred o'clock."

_____

_____

_____

_____

_____

_____

_____

_____

_____

_____

_____

_____

_____

_____

_____

_____

_____

_____

_____

_____

_____

_____

_____

_____
_____
_____
_____
_____
_____
_____
_____
_____
_____
_____
_____
_____
_____
_____
_____
_____
_____
_____
_____
_____
_____

Joy, trying her best to talk her way out of being punished, told her Daddy,
"I didn't really scream. I just kind of yelled."

Trish Lenzi

I was tying a bib onto Monica
before she ate her spaghetti, and she hollered,
"Mommy, you broke my neck!"

_____
_____
_____
_____
_____
_____
_____
_____
_____
_____
_____
_____
_____
_____
_____
_____
_____
_____
_____
_____

We had just recorded The Greatest Story Ever Told,
and Christa asked,
"Can we watch The Best Movie Ever Wrote?"

Two-year-old Josiah was yelling at birds to get off our porch, and his daddy chuckled, "We ought to call him 'Saint Josiah of Assisi!'"

Trish Lenzi

"Girls are a little pudgier than boys," Christa concluded, "because they have eggs in their bellies. Right?"

_____
_____
_____
_____
_____
_____
_____
_____
_____
_____
_____
_____
_____
_____
_____
_____
_____
_____
_____
_____
_____

While straining to peel her banana, Monica questioned,
"Are you sure this is a real banana?"

Trish Lenzi

_____
_____
_____
_____
_____
_____
_____
_____
_____
_____
_____
_____
_____
_____
_____
_____
_____
_____
_____
_____
_____
_____

*Six-year-old Joy was outside singing wholeheartedly,
"Lord Jesus, take me by the hand. Make me like a little child again."*

Christa wanted to know: "Mommy, are you right-handed or wrong-handed?"

"Joy is the best hair-do in the world," Monica announced.
Then she corrected herself saying, "I mean Joy does the best hair-dos in the world."

_____

_____

_____

_____

_____

_____

_____

_____

_____

_____

_____

_____

_____

_____

_____

_____

_____

_____

_____

_____

_____

_____

_____

Christa prayed,
"Thank you, Lord, for the nice day we had tomorrow."

_Not intentionally rhyming, I instructed Christa,
"Do what I say, right away, before you play, OK?"_

_____

_____

_____

_____

_____

_____

_____

_____

_____

_____

_____

_____

_____

_____

_____

_____

_____

_____

_____

_____

_____

_____

_____

_____

"Do you know what, Mommy?!" Joy exclaimed. "When aunt
Ruth takes a bath, she has none toys in with her!"

Christa asked, "Did God cook us when He made us?"

Trish Lenzi

Anytime someone called two-year-old Josiah "bad boy," he indignantly hollered, "I'm not a 'bad boy', I'm a 'dood boy'!"

Discussing instruments, Monica asked,
"Mom, are you good at playing the sympathizer?"

"Mommy," four-year-old Joy confided, "I really don't know who I should have for a boyfriend. Who should I marry?"

Wearing her favorite purple shirt, Christa questioned, "Can we get arrested if we don't wear red, white, and blue on the Fourth of July?"

"What kind of dog was Daddy's when he was little?" Monica wanted to know. "A leopard?"

_____
_____
_____
_____
_____
_____
_____
_____
_____
_____
_____
_____
_____
_____
_____
_____
_____
_____
_____
_____
_____
_____
_____
_____

"I wish I were a pig," Christa announced, "so I could play in the mud."

"Oh, good," Monica announced as she pulled her Daddy's flannel pajamas out of the laundry basket. "Dad said he was looking for his vinyl pajamas!"

The Palest Ink Is Stronger Than the Strongest Memory

"Hold my bubbie," Aaron said, handing Daddy his bottle. "But don't drink it."

_____
_____
_____
_____
_____
_____
_____
_____
_____
_____
_____
_____
_____
_____
_____
_____
_____
_____
_____
_____
_____
_____

*Two-year-old Joy saw some wrestlers on TV and commented,
"They're tickling each other."*

_____

_____

_____

_____

_____

_____

_____

_____

_____

_____

_____

_____

_____

_____

_____

_____

_____

_____

When I handed Monica a pair of pants to play in that had a few stains on them, she fussed,

"But, Mommy, these pants are a little bruised up."

_____

_____

_____

_____

_____

_____

_____

_____

_____

_____

_____

_____

_____

_____

_____

_____

_____

_____

_____

_____

I was taking two-year-old Joy to bed one night while my husband was watching a close basketball game on TV. He was hooting and hollering. Joy shook her head saying, " Daddy's the real silly man I ever saw in the world!"

After hearing a lady who played many different instruments, Monica shared,
"A lady in our Sunday School class plays all kinds of ornaments."

An ambulance went by, and five-year-old Christa exclaimed,
"There goes a boo-boo truck!"

Overhearing Joy instructing her one-year-old sister, Joy commanded,
"Christa, don't jibber-jabber, talk!"

I complained that the gums in the back of my mouth really hurt. Christa suggested, "Maybe it's your faithful teeth coming in."

One day, I discovered one-year-old Monica, sitting in the bathroom sink, chewing on everyone's toothbrush! Yuck!

_____

_____

_____

_____

_____

_____

_____

_____

_____

_____

_____

_____

_____

_____

_____

_____

_____

_____

_____

_____

_____

_____

_____

"Mom," Josiah announced, "when I get big and you get little,
I'm gonna punish you!"

_____

_____

_____

_____

_____

_____

_____

_____

_____

_____

_____

_____

_____

_____

_____

_____

_____

_____

_____

_____

_____

Aaron announced, "I'm a good listener to myself."

Trish Lenzi

"You know what would be good?" Aaron exclaimed.
"Chicken serenaded with ranch dressing!".

The Palest Ink Journal

You might want to consider self-publishing your own memories journal. It would make a wonderful gift for family or friends. CreateSpace is a self-publishing company that is very inexpensive. After you pay the initial fee, you can order just as many books as you want for a minimal fee. If you're curious, you can go to createspace.com for specifics. No pressure—just an idea.

Thanks for taking the time to read and write in The Palest Ink Journal.

Best wishes,

Trish Lenzi

www.ingramcontent.com/pod-product-compliance
Lightning Source LLC
Chambersburg PA
CBHW060923040426
42445CB00011B/771